MEDITATION – A FOUNDATION COURSE shows you a way of being still in the midst of the busy world. The lessons take you into meditation in easy stages and calm you down until eventually you can enjoy longer periods of more profound stillness. All the time you will know what you are doing and why.

Barry Long discards the religious, occult, or psychic traditions associated with meditation in the past. This is practical meditation, effective now. It is effective because the author has practised and lived what he teaches; the lessons have the authority of that self-knowledge.

Learning to meditate is often seen as a turning point, when life takes on new meaning. This book has introduced thousands of people to a better way of living. You too will soon discover the refreshing stillness and simplicity that is always available when you dissolve the tension of living.

MEDITATION
A Foundation Course
A book of ten lessons

BARRY LONG

BARRY
LONG
BOOKS

New revised edition 1995.
Reprinted 1995.

Barry Long Books are published by The Barry Long Foundation,
an educational charity registered in the United Kingdom.
Address: BCM Box 876, London WC1N 3XX

Text first published for private circulation 1969.
Booklet edition: The Barry Long Centre London 1982
reprinted 1983, 1984.
Revised edition: The Barry Long Foundation 1986
reprinted 1987, 1988, 1990, 1992, 1993.

British Library Cataloguing-in-Publication Data:
a catalogue record for this book is available from The British Library.

© Barry Long 1982, 1986, 1995.

Cover design: Rene Graphics, Brisbane, Australia.
Moon photograph: International Photographic Library.
Printed in England on acid-free paper by Redwood Books.

ISBN 1 899324 00 3

CONTENTS

Why? 1

How to use this book 2

Understand what you're doing 3

THE LESSONS

1 Posture, Breathing & the Still Mind 11

2 Meditating on the Body 25

3 Seeing the False 37

4 The Moment of Stillness 53

5 Self-Separation 69

6 Mastering the Mind 81

7 How to Deal with Worry 95

8 Meditation at Work 107

9 What is your Aim? 119

10 Signs of Deepening Awareness 131

What comes next? 141

The author and this book 145

BEFORE WE BEGIN

Why?

This book outlines an effective meditation method. It is a book about self-destruction. Meditation is destructive because it gradually dissolves the false in you – the false self you think you are, but are not. Precisely what this false self is you are going to find out.

When the false is destroyed you are what you are. What it means to be what you really are is beyond imagining and beyond anyone else's words or ideas. What can be said is that it is the peak of life – life's purpose for you, the individual, to experience as soon as you can.

This meditation answers a question that has puzzled men and women for thousands of years: why does the false, or what we know is not right, have to exist in us? The answer is: because it has purpose. The false in you, once it is seen, enables you to know the truth – just as a false promise when experienced reveals the value of what is true. Until you can recognise what is false you can't know what is real. Right from the start, meditation is an expanding vision of the real, the true.

The lessons that follow teach you how to start dissolving your false self – the essential foundation for discovering the truth which is yourself. To that end, to the truth you really are, this book is consciously dedicated.

How to use this book

The book is a course of ten lessons.

I suggest that after reading straight through, you thoroughly absorb each lesson in turn, say one a week – but taking longer if you feel you need it.

Read and re-read each lesson. But don't just read and recognise the truth of it: do it. The secret is to see for yourself what is true and to start living that immediately.

The book is short and to the point to help you absorb the whole idea of meditation easily and quickly and to apply it as a means to a better, more real way of living.

Every sentence means something. Nothing can be glossed over. Learn each lesson by practising what you are being taught before moving on to the next step.

For every lesson there is a set of exercises, appropriate for each stage of the course. They are written in abbreviated note form for easy reference and placed at the end of each lesson as an extra guide and reminder of the main points.

Please do the exercises and put the lessons into practice, step by step.

Understand what you're doing

The first object of meditation is to become the master of your mind. Anyone who worries has obviously not achieved this, for the peculiar symptom of worry is that even when you observe its stupidity and futility and resolve to stop, you cannot. It is the mind – your master – that worries, not you.

Everyone has mastered the mind to some degree. But as it is not a total control the effect is rather like claiming to be the master of a good dog that occasionally bites you. Obviously the mind does not want to be mastered so it is going to oppose you from the start. Recognise that fact now and you have already begun the battle by using your understanding.

Few people who begin meditation ever really succeed because they do not understand that the mind itself is the problem. Their methods, systems and teachers employ the mind to defeat the mind – a hopeless exercise. In this method you use a superior faculty, your understanding, plus a few devices to keep the mind doing what you want while your understanding of it grows. The principle is a simple one: what you understand you can control.

•

As understanding is the key to the method, you must not obey any instruction in this book without first understanding the reason for it, and relating it to your own experience to see that it makes sense. If you just obey mechanically you are being trained like animals that perform without understanding why. Your object is to become the master – and the master is the master because he or she understands why everything is being done.

•

Meditation will show you that worry is mechanical. Yet it is only one aspect of the mechanical in you. Anger, hate, arguing, envy, resentment, judging others, justifying yourself, blaming – all are mechanical; as are self-consciousness, fear and those two most painful lingering feelings, regret and remorse.

While the mind controls you, half your life is lost in mechanical ifs, shoulds, doubts and fears. You are trapped in a world of half-living, even though you are instinctively aware that something deep within you is mutedly crying out for release and expression.

The mind cannot find the key and finally – as countless others before you have done – you sigh: 'Where am I going? What's it all about?' And you get no answer. Even the genius and the millionaire are not spared.

•

A great deal of mumbo-jumbo has been written and talked about meditation.

To some meditation is almost a dirty word, to others a joke. To most it is as obscure and remote as medieval alchemy – the dabblers and quacks have seen to that, in the same way as down through the centuries they have always exploited self-knowledge with nonsense and mystification.

It is also worth pointing out that the saint is not necessarily a wise man, and the wise man is not necessarily a saint.

Much of what is said about meditation relates to a different subject – the psychic world. Meditation can and often does cause psychic experiences. But they are a by-product of a condition through which you must pass to find the truth of yourself. If you linger there or try to use the thoroughly unreliable and capricious forces of the psychic world, you will get no real answers, only more questions.

Some meditation techniques introduce emotional excitation or arousal – through visualisation, chanting, imaginative exercises, trance and so forth – but these will not get you real results, only more confusion. The reason is that whatever you project from yourself into the psychic world has to be returned to you sooner or later in another form; whereas in real meditation you are always with the new, never calling on or calling up the old.

Meditation is not dependent on body postures although it uses the body. Special physical exercises, breathing control and fasting are not necessary; although if you already practise these (and understand what you are doing) there is no reason to stop. If they are unnecessary or wrong for you they will drop away naturally as you proceed.

•

The opponent is the mind. It is your mind that worries and seethes with negative emotions; your mind that fails you by failing to observe its own mechanicalness.

It is the mind that makes the body smile while the mind plots treachery. Once the body is freed of the mind's wilful interference, it smiles and performs naturally.

You do not have to concern yourself with renouncing anything, with visiting another country or retreating into a forest or cave. Man's mind is where he is and that is where he must master it.

•

When you study any subject you are in a state of meditation – your mind is stilled on that subject to the exclusion of all other subjects. After you have studied or meditated on the subject for sufficient time, the knowledge you have absorbed crystallises into understanding and you no longer have to think to perform.

Such understanding in turn produces the still higher faculty of intuition. Depending on how much you love the subject you are studying, your knowledge of it becomes self-knowledge – for love brings union with yourself. Then, in the practice of it, you are able to perceive things not seen by others who only studied half-heartedly or because they had to. As this is true if you are learning for instance a language as the subject, so it is especially true when learning meditation – where you are the subject.

The more often you meditate on yourself and observe yourself in action, the stiller and more intelligently alert your mind will become. After a time you will find that many of the disturbing and destructive elements in your thinking have begun to disappear. You will find that you are experiencing more beauty and richness in your life – the kindly act, a deeper smile, the will to help someone without looking for acknowledgement, the lack of fear of tomorrow, and similar positive responses will be filling the vacuum left by the departing negative forces. You will begin to 'know' certain things that cannot be put into words. This is the dawning of the intuition of life – wisdom – brought about by increasing union with the subject being studied – yourself.

How long does it take to master the mind? About as long as it takes to master a foreign language. Success depends on the time and stillness you give to it. If you are half-hearted in the practice of the meditation exercises you will fail like the half-hearted student linguist.

LESSON ONE

LESSON ONE

Posture, Breathing & the Still Mind

The best times for meditation are first thing in the morning and last thing at night – say for ten or fifteen minutes a sitting. If there are likely to be interruptions or noise, use more convenient times.

Do not attempt to overdo things to begin with. Successful meditation depends on being relaxed and understanding what you are doing. Increase the duration and number of sittings as you feel it is right.

The only discipline is to be regular and not to consider whether you feel like it. At times the mind will not want to meditate – especially when you are making progress in stilling it. You may have to vary the times when you meditate but any excuse you make to yourself for missing out a sitting is false.

You can sit anywhere as long as you are alone. If one of your friends or family is learning with you, you can sit together, but this should be an extra period of meditation. You progress more quickly by sitting alone. The presence of another person will distract you; and you will find there are enough distractions in an empty, silent room without adding to them. Also, you may become dependent on company and be unable to meditate without it. Eventually you will find you can meditate anywhere, in the midst of bedlam if you are not physically involved, and still be able to keep your self-awareness.

•

Sit upright on a chair, with your back straight, feet together or a few inches apart and knees spread naturally. Hands can rest on the knees or thighs or be held loosely together on the lap.

Keep the skeleton upright.

Let the flesh fall, so that you are easy and not tense.

Hold the head erect.

Gaze straight ahead and close your eyes.

•

It is important to be comfortable and yet a little more aware of your posture than usual. If you are not comfortable the mind will keep darting away to the cause of the irritation instead of remaining where you want to put it. If your body is not more upright than usual you may go to sleep.

For some people, dropping off into a half-sleep is a problem. It is another example of our mechanicalness. But don't be discouraged. It usually disappears with practice. The mind is not used to being slowed down except when going to sleep and so it interprets meditation as the need of sleep. Again, it is the mind subconsciously controlling us. Avoid sitting down to meditate soon after a meal: a heavy stomach is an inducement to sleep.

Indian meditators sit cross-legged on the floor because that is the normal way of sitting in India. Like us they also face the possibility of falling asleep so they sit a little more erect in meditation. Some westerners, not understanding this, adopt the Indian posture as though it were essential to meditation. They struggle for months to overcome the discomfort of the unaccustomed position and having mastered it often regard this feat of self-control as an example of successful meditation. It is not. It is control of the body, not of the self.

The enemy of meditation is the mind. At this stage you cannot afford the time to stay and battle with the body. Battling involves training and training is mechanical. There is no dispute, nothing to prove. For the mind can win every time.

You close your eyes because it helps to stop the mind from racing. Things you see and hear remind you, by association, of other things. As these other things are in your memory you start thinking – and the mind has then taken over. You cannot close your ears nor shut off your senses of smell, taste and touch-feeling. But as the most distracting sense is sight, you can temporarily eliminate it by closing your eyes.

You are sitting up straight in the chair. Now close your eyes and take three or four slow, deep breaths.

These slow, deep breaths are to put the body at ease and stop the mind from trying to find the source of a new irritation, lack of oxygen. Whenever you attempt something new you tend to breathe shallowly. The body then does not get enough oxygen and becomes mildly inefficient. The mind, because of its lack of self-knowledge, will be unable to locate the trouble and its confusion will be felt as an inability to focus or apply yourself. For a person about to perform in front of an audience for the first time, the effect can be disastrous. The fear of failure adds to tension, the breathing becomes a flutter, an ineffectual pant, the body increasingly inefficient. The mind is unaware that its own anxiety is the cause. It races faster and faster down a panic spiral until it comes to a dead stop, fixed, not in freedom, but in terror, on its own self-consciousness. If the person starts performing mechanically he will have to take a breath that restores the respiratory cycle, thus getting through unconsciously.

You take these first deep breaths consciously, and then breathe deeply again every three or four minutes while you are sitting, or whenever you observe that your body needs another few deep breaths.

•

All you need now is something to direct the mind on to. This is usually the failure point of meditation methods. You need an object because it is impossible for the unmastered mind to be still and remain conscious without one. The mechanical mind can never rest – even in sleep it chatters on beneath the immediate awareness. It is thinking or engaged all the time.

If you close your eyes now and try not to think you will fail. Try it.

Within a couple of seconds the mind has begun associative thinking. That is, it hears, smells or feels something which reminds it of something in the memory and it races off along a line of related ideas or images. When you catch up with it again you will find it is a mile away from the first idea. If you put your attention on to a definite subject, the thinking will follow a more logical course; but the mind will not stay still, no matter what subject you fix it on.

•

Most people confuse a still mind with a blank, idiotic mind. Far from it. A still tiger is not a blank or idiotic tiger. A still mind and a still tiger are alert, aware, poised and ready.

In the East it is popular to put the mind onto a statue of the Buddha or some other formal aspect of the deity. But the problem then is that if the student does not have the statue with him, meditation becomes difficult. The mind begins to obey the presence of the statue as the performing lion obeys the sight of the whip. In the Himalayas there is an Indian who has been meditating for many years. From his small bungalow he has a view of the incredibly beautiful Himalayan snow-range: its grandeur and majesty stagger you every time you look at it. In front of this magnificent view he has put a grey concrete statue of a Hindu god to meditate on.

If the student tries to hold an image in his mind – as some schools teach – he will fail because the unmastered mind cannot hold on to any single image continuously. The only exception is when the mind is stunned by tremendous love or tremendous pain: then meditation is natural and continuous and no method is needed. Such cases involve great suffering and are rare.

Some religious teachers urge meditation on passages from the scriptures. This is effective if you truly love God and perceive the truth of the passages. But it is not a meditation method: it is an end in itself. Meditation is a means not an end.

Meditation is a road to somewhere – to an unshakeable state of being. The first tuition is how to get onto the road – how to still your mind. Then eventually the stillness becomes the whole natural state.

It is not uncommon for people to have moments of stillness, brilliant insights and revelations through means other than right meditation. But the moments are tantalisingly elusive, even for the most ardent seekers. This is because they have set out to find the road with a seeking mind instead of a still mind. While you seek anything before stillness you seek in vain. Stillness is the road.

The still mind does not have to seek or ask. It is already there, simultaneously at the beginning and the end. It just looks and sees what is.

In the next lesson we meditate on something that will lead to stillness and not to more thought. Since the mind starts to think by looking at objects outside yourself, to start stilling it you must turn and look within.

But first, go back over this lesson, and do it . . .

Make your commitment . . .

I'm sitting here to meditate.

There's nothing else I have to do or think about for the next ten minutes.

> *If there is, go and do it,*
> *or think about it.*
> *And then come back afresh.*

I know that any thought or restlessness that may occur in me is utterly false and comes from my mind.

I'm sitting here to meditate.

Take your seat on a firm chair.
Sit upright.

Keep the skeleton erect.
Let the flesh fall.

Close the eyes and breathe out until all the air is gone.

Breathe in slowly and gently and fill yourself with air.

Breathe out until you are empty.

Take three more of these deep breaths.

Deeply. Slowly. Evenly.

Now let the body breathe naturally.

Be still.

A thought comes in.

You're starting to think about something.

Observe yourself.

Thinking is mechanical.

Catch the thought.

And breathe out . . .

as if to breathe the thought away from you.

Breathe thoughts out!

LESSON TWO

Meditating on the Body

You begin meditating on the only object you cannot leave behind – your body.

Meditation is self-knowledge. At this stage you do not know the truth of what you are – but whatever you are, it is unarguable that you begin with your body. So that is where you begin meditation.

Sitting properly with your eyes closed and having taken a few deep breaths, you look at the feeling of your body. You look inwardly, using your inner attention.

First, the tip of the nose. Direct the attention onto it. Wait and see what you feel.

Just be aware of the feeling that is there. You do not look with the eyes open of course, nor do you move the hands.

You will notice that you do not have to think.

What is the feeling?

A tingling? A pulsing?

Whatever it is, the tip of your nose is alive.

•

Now go to the lips. There is certainly sensation there. Perhaps you notice the feeling is finer, more intense than the nose. Or is it? It's for you to say. It's your body. You're discovering it – in a new, conscious way.

Go to the feet. Feel the tingling there?

Go to the shoulders. Then the small of the back.

Take your time. Be sure to feel each part before you go on to the next. But if you can't feel one part after being still for a time, go on to another.

Now your knee joints and elbows. Less obvious, perhaps, but there is a feeling there. Not quite the same as the fleshy part, a feeling almost on the edge of pain.

•

You may feel a shiver up the back after a few attempts to look at your body. Everyone experiences these shivers, but people are seldom still enough or interested enough to watch them come and go, as you can now.

When the shiver comes, watch how the shoulders react as the spasm runs up through them; how the hair on the back of the neck and scalp tends to lift and how the final shudder runs back down from the tingling head like a receding wave.

The shivers tend to increase with meditation. Eventually they become a very fine feeling. The Indians associate the shudder with the rising of what they call the kundalini-shakti, the life-power that they say runs up the spine and through the brain into the frontal lobes; here it eventually stills the monkey-mind, so that the mind's incessant chatter is replaced by stillness and pure awareness. The energy is likened to a rising cobra, a serpent of wisdom, whose hooded head becomes a third eye of inner vision behind the centre of the forehead. This is a colourful explanation of what in fact you will experience sooner or later. Without the occult trimmings, you will be able to observe for yourself that the shiver-spasms occur more frequently as you progress; that they are later replaced by variations of the same phenomena, and that the moments and periods of great stillness and acute awareness continue to grow longer.

•

Observe your breathing. Notice how the rhythm can be impaired by your watching. Perhaps there is a connection here with the experience of the proficient pianist, typist or motorist who, when they try to think about the movements they are making, tend to become less efficient.

Next the heart. Where does it beat in your chest? Does the back of your head pulse with it? Or behind it?

You may notice the nostrils twitch. Later they may dilate and remain dilated for two or three seconds. This is the shakti power.

●

During each meditation you must look at yourself frequently to ensure that you are completely relaxed. You will not be, but the effect of observing tension in this way is to release it.

Tension gathers in us with the subtlety and certainty that dust gathers on a polished table.

The object is to watch what is happening in your body, not to make it conform to what you are reading here; nor to imagine things so that you deceive yourself. Your job is to stay the detached observer – as if someone had asked you to look into a room and report exactly what is going on in there. Only the facts are required.

●

Did you sway slightly – so that if you were to reflect on it, you would think it nothing, just an unconscious movement, if it happened at all?

In India, where it is difficult to do anything without an admiring audience turning up immediately, some gurus (teachers) forbid students to allow their bodies to sway in meditation when others are watching. The concern is that it may create a feeling of spiritual pride in the student. We are not concerned with that objection. The point is that the body does sometimes sway in meditation. Not everyone experiences it. If encountered, it should not be resisted, but observed.

The sway is usually from side to side and it can involve the whole trunk or merely the head. It can be quite pronounced or almost imperceptible and it is harmless. But you have to be watchful to see that you do not mentally keep the sway going when the originating impulse has ceased: the mind tends to do this. The real swaying stops abruptly and often leaves the body leaning off-centre, so that a deliberate act is required to bring it back to the vertical again.

•

There are many other part of your body to observe – the fingers, the soles of the feet, the armpits, the thighs, the gums. Even the teeth seem to be alive.

You may not get around all these parts of the body in the one sitting before the mind distracts you and carries you away. After four or five minutes your attention may not be able to reach the point you've decided on – as though there were an impenetrable barrier. There is. For example, if your attention is directed to the scalp, you may find the mind too busy thinking about the hairdresser for you to get through to it. If this happens and you are unable to get effective control, give up and do something else.

Do not sit and struggle with the mind: the force of its restlessness increases with opposition. The mind is reduced to obedience by your understanding of it: it has no defence against the stillness of understanding. Later, return to your meditation, relaxed and fresh.

•

You have launched the initial assault against the mind, a surprise attack, by making the mind co-operate in the observation of your body. Its counter-attack is to refuse to obey. After a few minutes of meditation it will insist on thinking about some other object or event. Do not be disheartened. Anything that can be made to obey for a few minutes can be made to obey forever.

Be patient. Keep working.

Close your eyes.
Put your attention inside your body.

See inside yourself.
Take a good look around.

What's happening?

Feel the feeling
  – in your fingers,
  – the tip of your nose,
  – lips,
  – feet . . .

There is a sort of tingling . . .

Can you feel all of them at once?
The sensation is different in different places.
It's not always easy to feel.
The sensation changes.

. . . a fine sensation.

Now go around the body, feeling the sensation.

What is the feeling
 – in your thighs,
 – elbows,
 – nape of the neck,
 – small of the back?

What do you feel?

If there is a response in the body, just observe it.

Put your attention into your shoulders.
Feel the tension there.
Allow the shoulders to drop down.

Let the tension fall.

Simply observe what is happening.

LESSON THREE

Seeing the False

To learn anything you have to meditate. The better you meditate, the better you learn. The principle is as simple as that.

When you learn anything you meditate on a subject outside yourself. When you learn or practise meditation the subject is yourself. In ordinary learning, say arithmetic, the subject is separate from us. We learn it by gradually absorbing the facts until the subject is a part of us, as our knowledge. In meditation the process is precisely the reverse. We begin with the subject – you – completely absorbed in itself, a fully-functioning human being. The process here is not to add to you, but to dismantle you; to separate all the knowledge you have acquired or learned from your real and precious self-knowledge. At present the two are indiscriminately tangled up. Let us now examine these two aspects of your knowledge. By simply doing that, we will start unravelling them and separating them out.

As astounding as it may sound, I cannot add one fact to your knowledge of yourself. I can tell you the facts of the atom, but the atom or any other subject is separate from you, so that would be ordinary learning. I cannot tell you that you can work miracles because you already know whether you can, as your own self-knowledge. Neither can

I tell you that you love your neighbour as yourself, for the same reason. I can tell you that you do not look well – because again that introduces another subject, your body. But I cannot tell you that you do not feel well; just as I cannot tell you whether you are angry or jealous, or innocent.

I cannot tell you that you desire to achieve something if you do not. I cannot tell you that you understand Russian if you do not. I cannot even tell you you're lying. You might deny it, but if it's a fact that you are lying I have not told you anything that you do not already know. If through this book you see anything new about yourself, I will still not have added anything to you. You will have just discarded your false knowledge – what you used to believe was true.

In other words, you are all there now, complete and perfect – underneath the garbage you have collected. The problem is not your practical knowledge or the facts you have acquired. It is something else that is always sneaking past your guard and getting added to yourself without conscious scrutiny – your impressions.

You have been under a constant bombardment of impressions since the day you were born. They are as subtle and imperceptible as breathing. And the disturbing truth, once you start facing it, is that most of them are false.

A youth observes the people around him and forms the impression that money is the key to happiness. So he devotes his life to becoming rich, only to discover as a wealthy man that it was a false impression.

A rich man forms the impression from the saints that poverty is the way to happiness and gives all he owns away – only to discover as a pauper that the impression was wrong.

On such foundations we have all built our personal selves and our personal worlds, each of us a collection of false impressions and mixed-up facts. Which is true and which is false? How can we judge? The very knowledge we use to judge with might itself be a part of the false in us.

Science went through the same crisis early this century. The physicists found that things were not working out. Two or three of them decided there was only one thing to do – to go back and re-examine the quality of the knowledge from which they were proceeding. It took courage and they were laughed at and misunderstood. But they worked on and on and eventually found that what for many years had been assumed to be true was no longer quite correct on the new threshold of discovery that science had reached.

Every physicist knew that Newton had defined the laws of gravity, and that they worked – to within an nth of a degree. But then Einstein threw the Newtonian concept out the window with a new formula that explained gravity in a new way and, what's more, removed the irritating nth degree of error. This, together with the other discoveries that gave science its new foundations on which to build the age of space travel, was made possible by a few men who had the audacity to question what everybody had previously accepted as true because it worked 'near enough'.

In this meditation we start checking for ourselves the validity of our own knowledge, all the facts we've been handed in packaged deals since we were children and have been using ever since as a 35-inch yardstick. As everyone uses the same measure, it's a cosy, comfortable compromise, at the distance we generally live from ourselves. But when you get up close to life, and begin asking questions, it just does not work out.

When a man or woman starts to ask themselves what life is about, they are ready, like the physicist, to step out of the slow old world of effects into the flashing new world of causes where near-enough knowledge or warped measuring sticks are not good enough.

For instance, when you start to look for yourself, you might discover that the impression of what it is to be selfish, which was handed down to us and which we have handed on to our children, is quite wrong. You might discover that to be selfish is to expect something from somebody – or anything from anybody. In which case, whenever you call someone selfish in the accepted sense of the word, you yourself might be being selfish.

A lot of self-shaking can occur in the changing of the simplest attitudes. You might also discover that humility is not the exclusive possession of the saint, who lives without having to raise a family in a nine-to-five scramble on just enough money for it to be not enough. You might find that being humble is an inner thing that requires no show and valiantly accepts all that life dispenses – always rising above the mechanical desire to blame another or look for sympathy. You might even discover that you've been conned by all the others who were also conned before you into believing that life is a battle with things outside ourselves. You might discover that as we win the battle within ourselves we win the battle of life without.

If you do not know these things, what will you do if they turn out to be true? You will have to discard as false many of the assumptions on which you have based your way of life.

Some impressions we receive are very pleasing – like being told we are honest, brave, clever, loyal. Although we do not lap it all up, we like to imagine we are most of these things. They are not facts of you, however, or they would be true of you all the time. You may be honest more often than you are dishonest, but these impressions are essentially hit-and-miss measurements. And how we treasure them! Just let someone accuse us of being dishonest, disloyal, cowardly or stupid – and we react. We react because the person is trying to take away from us a quality we really believe is ours, like our impression of ourselves as honest. You are only honest at the moment you are conscious of the opportunity of being dishonest. Otherwise it is not worth mentioning – and we don't, do we?

So I cannot take away from you any basic impression that you have acquired of yourself – without risking an argument. How then do we get rid of what is false in you? And who is to say what is false and what is not?

A normal person who treasures an object as being genuine and then discovers it is a fake will discard the object or lose interest in it. There is often a haste to be rid of it, followed by a feeling of relief, or even freedom. In short, you cannot cherish or cling to what you know is false. This remarkable truth is essential to the next exercise: it will serve you perfectly by sorting out what is true and what is false in you without any choosing or decisions on your part.

All you have to do is be conscious enough, often enough, to observe your impressionable self in action.

At present when you see yourself being angry, moody, cruel, dishonest, insincere, vindictive or vain, you do nothing effectual about it. Feeling guilty, ignoring it or deciding to try to change, changes nothing. So you continue the way you were. But from now on, while you practise this meditation, it is going to be different. You are going to see yourself in the moment of being angry, resentful, disagreeable and so on.

Just as you have learned to be conscious and observe your body sensation, so you are to observe these negative feelings as they arise in yourself, and watch their effects as your actions.

You will be observing yourself within and without simultaneously.

It is crucial that you do not get drawn in and lost in the feeling or action you are observing. You must remain the uninvolved observer. You do this by not condemning what you see, not excusing it or justifying it to yourself or anyone else. This is the key. Neither do you turn away from it in distaste. You observe it.

You must not try to correct or change anything. Just observe what is happening.

Do this as often as possible and what you observe in yourself – if it is false – will slowly drop away. What is true will remain untouched. As anger, resentment, moodiness, vanity, guilt, cruelty, dishonesty, vindictiveness, insincerity and all the rest of these emotional reactions are false, they will begin to vanish. Know that only the detached observer, the pure intelligence in yourself free of acceptance or rejection, can do it.

After a time of practising this you will feel pain, as though a part of you were dying. If you look closely at this you will see that it is a kind of emotional death. The pain will be coming from the mind's attempt to cling and hold on to that false part of your self which is dissolving. If you are valiant, you will bear the pain and let the false part die. If you are not, you will make a perfectly logical excuse that everyone will agree with – except the part of you that yearns to be free.

When the false part dies there is a reward like that of the heartbroken lover who suddenly in the midst of his (or her) agony sees that he is free of the other – that he would not, could not have her back; that he is experiencing freedom, not in hate but in knowing that clinging to love is a false dead thing, kept alive only by the fear of losing.

※

At this stage,
give twice the time
to sitting in meditation.

Look at yourself in a mirror.
See yourself as you are.

Watch yourself.

Watch as thought tries to come
between you and your reflection.

Blink.

Blink to break up your concentration
and to relax your eyes.

The exercise is to observe your own reflection
without making any mental comment.

Just see.

Situation: a conversation with your partner or a relative.

Take the opportunity to quietly observe your reactions to what is being said.

How many assumptions are you making?

No expectations.

Situation: on a bus, in a queue or in the street
you overhear strangers talking.

Observe your curiosity.

The exercise is to restrain yourself
from getting imaginatively involved
with people and events.

No comment.

Observe how often at home and at work
you make an excuse for something you've said or done.

Silent excuses also count.

No excuses.

In sitting meditation, you may find yourself thinking
about someone you know.

If you love the person, and you feel that love in you,
the thinking will not go on.

More likely, you will be thinking about a demand
you are making on the person or that is being made on you.
You will be liking or disliking him or her.
You will be discussing your opinions with yourself.
You will not be sitting in meditation but in judgement.
And the thinking will go on and on and on.

Observe this taking place in your own experience.

See the false – but don't try to change things.

No judgements.

LESSON FOUR

The Moment of Stillness

The purpose of meditation is to find the stillness within you. This initially may be a brief experience in which the mind slows noticeably; or it may even stop for a second or two. Either experience is dramatic. And do not think afterwards that you might have imagined it. That will be the mind trying to shake your confidence.

The length of time it takes to achieve either of these moments depends on the individual. Some people will discover they have been meditating in a way for years without realising it. But by going about it deliberately like this they will experience the slowing down of the mind, or the stillness, much more quickly. However, no matter how proficient you seem to become at falling straight into a stillness, do not neglect the technique of going around the body with your inner attention. This requires a deliberate act, an exercise in obedience for the mind. And once you have mastered the technique, you will find it results in a distinct slowing down and quite often a stop.

To ignore the body procedure and fall straight into an imagined stillness is inadvisable. You fall into a half-daze; you are only half-conscious and mistake this pleasant semi-sleep for successful meditation. This is a mind trick. The unfailing test of successful meditation is to be present in your body where your body is; not to be absent in some sort of trance or thought-world.

You are aware of everything that is going on within you as the feeling of yourself. If anything happens outside you that you need to know about, you feel it instantly. Without trying, you are present within and without. It is a state of acute awareness, of maximum consciousness.

•

As you become familiar with meditating at home you should find yourself beginning to meditate wherever and whenever you are unoccupied. So far we have only practised sitting in meditation. But meditation can be practised while standing; or lying down – in bed or bath; even while walking.

There is work to do on yourself every second that you are not actively engaged in normal duties. More and more you will find your meditation fitting into your everyday life, with your new awareness informing whatever you do. There is no reason why you should not go into meditation standing up in a busy train. Or sitting on the bus. Or waiting for someone on a street corner. You may hear a passing child say 'Look mummy, that person's asleep standing up!' (The children, like our minds, think we close our eyes only to go to sleep.)

•

Why is meditation so centred on stillness?

Because stillness is behind every creative and meaningful thing you do. If you are a scientist, or a plumber, and want to solve a problem – the scientist to see whether an experiment works, or the plumber to find the cause of a water failure – what do you do first? You go still.

You look at what's happening, or what has happened, in front of you. You look. And to look, to see, you have to go still. You can't perceive unless you're still. You don't reason or think. That comes after. First you observe the problem in stillness – and out of that stillness you then draw a conclusion or possible solution, and go into action. But stillness comes first.

•

Stillness pervades everything that moves.

Take the example of the universe. If you want to see the great mass of the universe direct, you go outside on a clear night and look at the starry heavens.

What do you see in the heavens?

You are actually looking at stillness. You are still and so is the starry universe.

What makes the clear night sky so beautiful, majestic, penetrating?

Its stillness – and yours.

It's the same when anything beautiful, arresting or dramatic catches your attention; at that moment, as you gaze at it to know it, you are still. So you must be still to start to know and perceive the wonder of yourself within.

Meditation is learning to consciously hold the stillness – and with it you hold the wonder.

Now put meditation into your daily life.

. . . On your way to work.

. . . Doing the washing up.

. . . When you get into bed tonight.

Take your attention around the body.
Attend to the breathing.
Relax the shoulders.
Feel the sensation in your hands, feet,
or wherever your attention goes.

Situation: you have a practical problem to work out
or some unfamiliar task to perform. Perhaps it's how to use
a new household gadget or how to assemble something.

Observe yourself as you go into action.

Look at the problem.
Don't think.
Stick to the facts in front of you.

Pause.

Now act.

Situation: you are very busy.
The phone rings.

Let it ring.
Pause.

Breathe out fully.
Breathe in gently.

Reach for the phone.

Situation: there is something you have to do
and it must be done immediately – done now!

Stop.
First drop your tension.
Then do it.

Remember:
  Stop.
  Drop.
  Go.

Nothing is more important than a moment for yourself.
So make the moment – put in the pause.

Stillness comes first.

Watch for moments of stillness.
In a scene of beauty.

Or in a moment of surprise or shock.

Listen for the silence
in between the sounds.

Everything sits in space.

See the space between the furniture.

See the space between the stars.

When the moon is in the sky
stand outside, in the still of the night,
and gaze upon the moon.

Feel the sensation in your body.
Don't let your mind move.

See the beauty
and know that the moon
is a mirror in the sky
of the beauty in you.

LESSON FIVE

Self-Separation

The secret of meditation is in self-separation. This leads to a totally new state of self-integration. As you follow the teaching in these lessons you are learning to separate out the observer – your consciousness – from the false in yourself. After enough practice of self-separation, the false is exposed, cannot stand alone and so vanishes. You then realise that the observer, the body and the still mind – you – arc a fully integrated, harmonious whole. No longer is there any separation.

However, until you reach that point you will keep getting tangled up with the emotions of the false self acting through your body and mind. You will experience periods of confusion and self-doubt and you will lack any permanent, real feeling of yourself. That is why it is essential, at this stage, to practise self-separation.

The separation is not spatial or physical. It is an intensification of the process you have already begun, the process of becoming more conscious by consciously observing your body and mind in action. The mechanics of it are simple. And you should understand them.

There is the observed and there is the observer. When you sit and meditate on the body (Lesson Two) the body is the thing observed and you are the observer. When you observe something false in yourself (Lesson Three) it is the emotion, habit or attitude that is the observed – and the observer is your true self, the you that knows the truth because it can distinguish the false. By being the still, detached observer of the observed, you are separating your self out.

•

At times, when you are endeavouring to keep the mind still, it races off to some thought, or slips into day-dreaming; but in a fleeting instant, you see what's happening. In that split-second you recover your consciousness and separate from the momentum of the mind. You are present. You are where you are, without thought. And you are able to watch the thinking mind as separate from yourself.

The aim is to make that instant of consciousness longer and longer, so that there is no thought – and finally to make it a permanent, complete and unmistakable state.

Meanwhile the task is to remember to be conscious!

•

Most people live their lives completely identified with their thinking, their body and their emotions. The only time they experience self-separation is in moments of shock, great pain or anguish. Then the separating is done unconsciously. And because it is not voluntary, it is of little value; seldom does anything lasting and worthwhile come out of it.

However, when you have to face these moments, as everybody does sooner or later, try to remain present and use the experience. You are likely to be reminded of this teaching at that moment; so use it, by staying conscious.

If you have already experienced something like this, you will know how trivial are the reactions of the mind and emotions compared to the reality you face at that moment.

•

As you practise self-separation you will begin to realise the truth of your mind – by understanding it. You will discover increasingly that direct experience alone, your own experience of the mind now, is of real value. Other people's theories and opinions about the mind are useless.

It is not advisable to be drawn into discussions and speculation. You will discover the truth for yourself, without ever having to discuss or debate what it is. Theories are about the experience of the mind, its ceaseless movement, and that is not the truth. The truth is the stillness of the observer that sees the movement.

•

The next exercise is to practise separating while you are walking.

Observe whether you have your head down. A person walking with the head down is usually thinking and unconscious of himself and life around him. Walk with your head up, deliberately. Or with your head down – but do it deliberately.

Observe the way your feet fall. Do not look down. You might find that the left foot turns in more than the right, or vice versa.

Do not try to change anything. You are only observing what is.

In the beginning, your conscious observation may interfere with the smooth flow of the body movements. Let the body be. Keep observing and it will correct itself; and gradually walk in the way you feel is right. If you do not interfere, but just keep observing, you will find that what is right for the body is what you are feeling and what you are feeling is right for the body. This is a form of integration – body and consciousness working in unison, or as one.

Observe how your left arm swings in unison with the right leg. How the faster you walk the more you shorten your neck.

Do you slouch along? It does not matter. You are only observing. But one thing is certain: if you catch yourself walking round-shouldered often enough, and you feel it is not right for you, your body will gradually correct it. Any posture that is not right, that is false, and which you continue to observe in yourself, will change. It is not changed by some mental resolution. It is changed by the simple act of observing yourself without thought. But you must be present: your consciousness as the observer must be there. Without that, no worthwhile permanent change is possible.

Walking meditation . . .

Observe the action of your arms and legs,
the way your feet fall,
the position of your neck.

Be easy.

Pick a route that you regularly use
– to the shops, to the bus,
down the corridor at the office –
and every time you walk that way this week,
remember to be conscious of where you are.

Stay conscious.

What is it that is walking?

The body.

See this.

Meditate at meal-times . . .

Give up thinking while you are eating.
Observe the actions of your hands and your mouth.

Observe the way you lean forward to the meal.
Do you have a tendency to grab and snap at the food?
Or to play with it?

Look at the food.
Take a pause
before taking a bite.

Taste the flavours.
What is doing the tasting?
Your appetite or your body?

When you take a hot drink,
let your body feel the warmth of it.

When you eat fresh fruit,
look for where the sweetness is.

Situation: the discussion of some 'important' issue.
It may even be a 'spiritual' subject.
You may or may not be participating.
You may just be watching a debate on TV.

Observe what happens within yourself,
as your mind registers the arguments
and you begin to join in with your own opinions.

Notice the mind's momentum.
See it in the others.
And see if it is in you.

Stop! As you are!

Hold yourself in that position.
Sitting or standing.

Hold the position.
Keep holding it.

See yourself – as in a freeze-frame photo.
Someone stopped the movie.
You're stuck in a fixed position.

> *There's nothing to think about.*
> *Just be here.*

Do not consider, 'How long have I been like this?'
Nor, 'How long will it continue?'

Just watch.
Moment to moment.

> *I'm doing this because I want to.*
> *But it might change any moment.*

A moment comes when the body moves.

> *The thinker is not the body.*

LESSON SIX

Mastering the Mind

The mind cannot be defeated by opposition. It always wins because whatever notion or attitude eventually triumphs is still a notion or attitude of the mind. It was the mind battling with the mind. You cannot win such a battle. The real battle – which you can win – is for you to remain the observer.

To observe the mind, first go around the body as I have described. This will always settle you down.

Take some deep, slow breaths. Be easy.

Now watch the thought that comes into your mind. Do not try to stop it. Endeavour to observe it. If the observer is fully present, thought cannot come in. And you will be thoughtless, still – until you lose your presence or consciousness, and start to think.

•

You may be able to stay conscious – thoughtless and present – for a second or two. If it is longer, all the better. But then you will identify with the mind, lose your status as the observing intelligence, and race off along a thought-line. Even so, don't be discouraged. Twenty to forty associated mind pictures later, you will become aware of why you are sitting there; you will separate from that thought-line, go still and recall your object – which is to be the observer.

Notice that you have control of the mind as long as you can observe and hold the first idea or thought-picture that comes in. While you hold that first picture, the mind cannot move and you are then separate from it.

You may actually feel the mind's frantic struggle to present the next associated picture – a real compulsion to think – before you are again swept along with it and immersed in its flow of moving pictures, like a phantom audience in a phantom cinema.

•

Think of the face of someone you love – and hold it.

You cannot do it for long. The image moves and starts doing something. Or it changes to a location or person associated with her or him, and so on.

If you try to hold the image of the moon, the same thing happens.

When you can hold the original image, you deny the mind its momentum. The mind depends on momentum for its stability, its forceful control of you. It's like a moving bicycle; as it goes faster the bike becomes more stable in itself. Without momentum, both the bicycle and the mind are powerless.

Eventually, when you are able to hold one image (or no image) for as long as you wish, the mind will give up. It will lie down like an obedient dog and await your command. Then, when you want to use the wonderful abilities of the mind for some practical purpose, you simply focus on the problem, and like a true master standing in the background you watch it – making sure, of course, that it uses only facts, not impressions. When the mind has done its job, it stops immediately – thoughtless, alert and still, waiting for your next command.

•

In those intervals when you're free of the mind's ceaseless chattering – which may only be short at first – you will be in the intensely aware present. You will hear the birds sing, see the grass between the paving stones, smell the sweetness of the breeze and listen to the song of life that never stops, even in a busy office – while others around you hear only the tumult and clamour of their own troublesome minds.

The next exercise will also help you to master the mind. Remember, the mind is only able to be master of you because you're ignorant of how it works, and because you don't see what tricks it gets up to.

After you have lost yourself in a thought-line and then recovered your presence, work back from where you stopped thinking, association by association, to the original thought or picture that started you off. If you started off thinking about a friend and came out of it down by the river where you once had a picnic, track back from the river, through all the associated images, to the initial thought of the friend.

Surprisingly, this is not hard to do. This is real meditative work and the more you practise, the more the mind will co-operate. The mind is a superb instrument and its greatest delight is to work properly. It respects and responds to firm direction. But for a while, like a dog in training, it will get diverted on the way back and race off along another thought-line. When you catch up with it again, track back from there. Forget about the old diversion. Always track back along the new one – and don't be anxious about running out of tracks!

For a time you will seldom get back to the thought that started you off. But persevere. Be vigilant to ensure the mind has not found a way to trick you. The mind will not be mastered by a fool. Right to the end it will use its cleverness and cunning to test you. Watch for its tricks. For example, it will wait until you are sitting in meditation and then remind you that it is imperative, at this moment, to think about a particular person or a bill you have to pay. Of course, it's not important at all, let alone imperative – or you would not have sat down to meditate.

Occasionally, instead of tracking wearily back from half-completed thought-lines, wipe off everything and begin again. Get up and walk around for a few minutes. Then sit, take your deep, slow breaths and start afresh. There is no need to made a drudgery of it.

Vary the exercise. Try to hold a particular image; and after you lose it, track back.

Or wait for a thought to come in and then track back immediately to whatever triggered it. Every thought has to have had a trigger.

Or, when a thought comes in, pin it. Hold it as long as you can.

●

You will notice in meditation that thoughts are often triggered by a sound – a voice, a creak, an aircraft, a car horn. This throws up an image out of the memory and the mind races off from there. If you become alert to it soon enough, you will be able to track quickly back to the external stimulus, and be conscious where you are now.

Notice with your eyes open that the mind reacts to a continuous stream of visual thought-triggers. Uncontrolled or unengaged, the mind never stops wandering.

The source of some thoughts cannot be traced. They rise from emotions you have buried in yourself and have not faced. Other thinking comes from sex. Sooner or later you will have to deal with those levels of yourself. That is outside the scope of this book (I have written other books and made tapes to take you further). For the moment, the task is for you to slow down the thought-machine, begin to get control of it, and then discover stillness.

•

Stillness of the mind may come to you in one of two ways. In the first, you discover that the final thought-image grimly being held has dissolved, and that there is no longer anything on the screen of the mind. It – or you – are unbelievably still. This can be quite a surprising experience and there may be the feeling that the stillness was there for some time before you became aware of it.

The other way stillness comes is by keeping out thoughts, or seeming to throw them out as they occur. However, what you are actually doing here is dissolving thoughts. You are dissolving them with the power of your conscious presence. Look closely. You will see it is effortless.

The feeling of keeping thoughts out is the pressure of thought activity on the perimeter of your stillness, which will quickly widen with practice.

•

Thoughts are all independent images. Unless the mind that links them into a continuity is stilled, the images cannot be separated.

The thoughts are carried on waves formed from the emotional and sexual levels of yourself. That's why the feeling of thinking is one of momentum. Also, you will notice that the waves are at their strongest, or most worrying, when the emotions and desires are aroused. But

once you are able to get between the thought-images by
separating them out as you are learning to do, the waves
start to lose their force and their ability to worry or control
you.

The observer is your awareness.
The observed is an invading thought.

Witness the invasion of thought.

When your awareness is fully present,
there is no thought.

Is that true?

Catch yourself thinking.

The thoughts are moving pictures.
Slow the movement.

Seize one of the pictures.
Hold it still.

The object of the exercise is to catch
the first thought-picture that comes.

Next time, be swifter . . .

You catch yourself thinking.
You swiftly seize and hold the image
of what you were thinking about.

Now track the thought-line back.
Image by image.
Not missing a single one out.
Nor spending longer on one than another.

Work back towards the initial thought.
Be aware of the diversions on the way.

Mastering the mind is like training a dog.

Situation: sitting in meditation.

There's a noise in the room
or in the street outside.

A car is passing . . .
Don't let your imagination drive off.

> *Let the sound pass through you.*

The clock is ticking . . .
Don't count the ticks.

Don't join the noise outside you.

> *Let it all happen in your stillness.*

LESSON SEVEN

How to Deal with Worry

When you are worrying and cannot stop, your mind is mastering you. But no one worries continuously. Worry comes in waves. So when you are worried, sit as usual, take some deep breaths, go around the body for steadiness and observe what is happening. Try to isolate the first image that comes in; and hold it as long as possible. Then, after you have lost yourself in thought and recovered from it, back-track if you can.

You will have to work harder at remaining conscious or present. The waves carrying the worrying thoughts will be very strong. You are likely to be doing a lot of huffing and puffing as the mind rebels; it wants to quit trying to be conscious and get on with the worry unimpeded. But you should now have the control to keep separating from the thought-line, pulling back to yourself – even though you soon end up identifying with the worry again.

To remember to separate is the thing. There is the worry, which is the thoughts; and there is you, the observer. You are not the same.

What counts is the number of times each minute, hour or day that you remember to separate; not how long you may think you hold each separation.

Do not get disheartened. It is difficult. But while you continue, even though you seem to fail so often, you are winning – gaining in consciousness.

•

Worry always accompanies a sense of loss or defeat. If it accompanies an anticipated loss or defeat, it is fear. The loss will seem very personal but it will be observed to fall into one of these categories: loss of power, position, prestige, possessions, permanence (health) or a person. To lose any of these is to lose part of yourself – and it hurts.

The seeming magnitude of the loss is irrelevant. To some people the loss of their good name means more than the death of their child. Values vary with the individual. One thing that does not vary is the feeling of loss and the weight of the sorrow that follows.

As meditation digs some depth in you, it will deepen your capacity for sorrow. But it will be a sorrow that does not depend on 'me' and 'mine'. This sorrow – it is really a deep, deep longing for what cannot be named – is the beautiful in man and woman and its dawning is an awakening.

Meditation slowly removes the feeling that you lose anything – and so it eventually rids you of all worry. And it transforms lingering sorrow into love.

Let me remind you how meditation does this. It removes the false in you by allowing you to consciously see the false. When you consciously see the false in yourself you discard it. Underneath the false – beneath the rubbish – is your true being. And in your true being is that wonderful feeling that everyone without exception longs for and seems to have lost consistent touch with – love.

Worry is false. But it is not good enough for you to just be told so, or to know it and not be able to stop it. You have to feel the pain of it. And you have to see it as false in yourself – in the midst of your worry, not afterwards. Everyone knows afterwards that worry is stupid, but they worry again. It doesn't matter how much you want to believe that worry is false, or say you know that it is false, you'll go on worrying. Like everything else false, worry is only overcome by understanding it in the moment that it is active, there, performing in you.

To understand anything you have to watch it work, examine it, and if possible get inside it; be there when it is born.

If you meditate regularly and earnestly you will find yourself separating naturally. In the midst of worry there will be strange, still interludes. This separation is the unmistakable sign of progress.

•

Worry arises out of self-interest. Nothing is wrong with self-interest. Without it we would be useless to anyone or anything and we would die. But worry is false self-interest because it contains no intention of action.

Genuine self-interest results in action – irrespective of whether the action is good or bad. False self-interest does not. Worry never contains the intention to act because it never has a genuine object. It is unconscious – deliberate self-delusion, aimless movement, all inside the head.

Here again you must beware of the mind's trickery. The worried mind will try to make out that it's exploring the possibilities of action. But it is not. You should observe for yourself that the moment you plan a genuine course of action to retrieve a position, you have to stop worrying.

Planned action requires aim. It demands a straight, cohesive thought-line of understood facts leading up to the action. You are too engaged in assembling the facts to worry; and later, too busy putting them into action. You reject impressions. They are false – the stepping stones of worry. And because they are false they will not stand up to your conscious scrutiny.

The test for yourself is: Do I genuinely intend to act on the thought-line I am following? If not, give it up. Be honest, be strong.

If you are desperate for money and decide to rob a bank, you will not worry while you are intent on action. You might be nervous; but nervousness is not worry. Once the decision is made, you will deal only in the facts which in your assessment will bring about a successful raid. But if you think about robbing the bank knowing that you have no intention of doing it, your mind will refuse to work effectively for you. It will play around with impressions – unworkable, useless daydreams or fanciful imagination. This is the seemingly harmless side of the terrible coin of worry.

•

Observe that the self-delusion in worry gives your mind a vicious sideways twist. Instead of thinking straight, it tears around in a circular thought-line, always ending up back where it started – on loss, helplessness, or grief – and never on what can be done now.

Observe that if you can hold the first image in worry, you're not able to go on worrying. You may still feel the loss or sorrow as a certain heaviness, like a black cloud in the background, but you will not have thought with it – a strange experience indeed for any man or woman used to the habit of lying awake worrying.

Obviously it is not easy to pin and hold the mind still like this while the emotions are disturbed. It is not achieved by a couple of efforts at meditating on worry. It comes from persistent practice of every exercise in this book – devotion to your aim.

If you can't stop thinking in the good times,
you'll certainly find it hard in the bad times.

You have various routines that excite your mind.
Such as:
    – reliving conversations you had today,
    – thinking about last night's TV show,
    – daydreaming about money, holidays, possessions and sex,
    – mentally going over the events of the day
      when you're lying in the bath or in bed at night.

Observe yourself performing these routines.

Why am I indulging my mind like this?

See how fleeting and second-hand the pleasure of it is.
See how rapacious the mind is. How it lusts for the past.

How much of my thinking is really necessary?

See that all this aimless mental activity wastes your vitality.

Situation: walking along the street.

Some people have a tendency to read all the shop-signs
and read the advertisements.
Do you do it?

Do you inwardly name and label
all the things around you?

If you do, observe how it places a screen
between you and your experience.

And notice how much less you do it
in the country, among natural things.

Man-made things are made by minds
and make you think.

Test this for yourself.
It may not be true.

Situation: you have a problem.
You've been thinking about it and got nowhere.
So, get hold of the main thought; the one that keeps recurring.
Fix your attention upon it.
Now ask yourself:

> *How many times have I already*
> *thought about this?*

Next, review the facts.

> *What is the situation?*

Look to see if any action can be taken.

> *Do I genuinely intend to act?*

If there's something you can do . . .

> *I'll do it now.*

If there's nothing to be done . . .

> *Why do I go on thinking about it?*

If there are several possibilities,
therefore uncertainty, therefore confusion . . .

> *What do I want?*

If you don't know, get hold of the feeling of wanting something.
It is a feeling somewhere in your body.
There's nothing else to do for now.

> *Give up the thought.*

Increase the time you give each day
to sitting in meditation.

The times of deep worry,
when the mind is desperate,
are the times to use everything
you have learned so far.

Your meditation seems to fail you.
You cannot stop the thoughts.
Then remember this:
> *With every attempt I gain in consciousness.*

And remember:
There is the worry.
And there is your body.
They are not the same.
> *I am not the worry.*

LESSON EIGHT

Meditation at Work

You must learn to meditate when conditions are noisy and not helpful. You start by observing your actions and mind while you are at work or engaged in something, such as a hobby, that you know you do well. You are then efficient and that usually means you enjoy what you are doing.

As you observe yourself working and being efficient you will see that your trouble-free performance depends on your being in control of yourself and not distracted. In fact you will notice that what at other times would distract you, does not distract you.

Distractions are false. Noise and unhelpful conditions are distractions when your mind makes an excuse of them – for being angry, impatient or sharp with others, for instance.

The more you observe yourself performing easily and efficiently the more you will associate with that trouble-free state. And the easier it will become for you to perform in that way whatever you are doing, even if the conditions are noisy and unhelpful. So when the time comes and you have to sit in meditation in difficult conditions, you will have prepared yourself.

•

The difficulty while you are busy working at your job or hobby is to remember to separate. However, by now you should have started to catch yourself observing yourself in action – without having to remember. This might occur only once or twice a day, and the rest of your separating might depend on the effort to remember (and even that without much success). But effortless separating is what you are after. Once it starts, it keeps coming.

There is no ten-day or even ten-month course in meditation that can cut corners for you. By now you will know how difficult it is to become conscious even for a few seconds a day. It is no easier for anyone else. But every inch you gain is gained forever. Every foothold is the sure ground of the next faltering step.

•

While you are being efficient in your work, endeavour to observe the following:

You are not aware of any tedious effort. You can whistle, hum, sing or even pause for a joke without interfering with the continuation or quality of the work.

You do not think. You act with a thoughtless awareness that moves with logical precision from fact to fact, action to action, moment to moment, towards the aim of the work.

Your mind is transparent, still, alert – but occupied like the surface of a lake over which the wave of pure action rolls effortlessly.

If a difficulty suddenly arises, you do not worry. You respond by acting or planning a new course of action. If you cannot act immediately, you look for more facts and wait, or do something else until the information arrives.

If you do worry, and are later able to meditate back on what happened, you will discover that you substituted concern for yourself for concern for the job – you confused the aim. Furthermore, your colleagues or superiors will accuse you of panicking or being unable to cope. And if they remain efficient in such an emergency they will push you aside and take over the action.

When you remain efficient in the face of an obstacle you face it squarely and pull out of your memory the facts you know from experience will counteract or remedy the situation. Only as a last resort will you act on impressions or suppositions. If forced to act on them, you will be acutely aware of their unreliability and will announce your doubts or dismay at having to use them.

Compare all this with how you approach the problems in your love-life and personal relationships. Do you begin to see why they invariably go wrong?

※

Perform an activity you enjoy and do well.

Observe your body in action . . .

- free of effort,
- thoughtless,
- alert,
- responsive.

Your aim – to make the whole of life like this.

Feel the tension in your shoulders.
Drop the shoulders.
Let it all go.

Breathe out.
Expel all the old air.

Breathe in new air.
Feel it in your nostrils.
Feel it pervade your body.

Breathe out slowly.
Wash the tension away with the breathing.

After closing your eyes for a while
look into the middle distance.

Now let the field of vision extend
to the corners of your eyes.

Take the strain out of seeing.
Blink.
Blink slowly.
Blink deliberately, to ease the eyes.

Whenever you find you're concentrating on something,
notice the hardness, the narrowness of your vision.
Then pull back the focus of your eyes.

Break your concentration.

Practise pulling back in the eyes:

Focus on an object in front of you;
at the same time look out of the corners of your eyes.
Notice that your attention has shifted to the middle distance.

Feel how this takes the strain and concentration out of
looking, yet you are fully aware.

Now the next step:
Pull back to the middle distance,
then draw further back
along the line of sight
until your eyelids close
and your attention is drawn back
within the forehead.

The eyelids may flicker slightly.
These are the energies within the face.
Wherever there is sensation, enjoy it.

Pulling back in the eyes can be used as a way
of directing your attention back within the body
– especially useful at the beginning of a meditation.

You've observed the effort that usually goes into seeing.
Notice how the same effort goes into hearing.

Can you pull back the focus of your ears
and listen with less effort?

Give up the trying.

Deliberately meditate in unhelpful conditions.

When there is impatience,
face the fact of the situation.

Use the breath to expel irritation.

See through the conditions.
They will pass.

Look for the good.
The good remains.

LESSON NINE

What Is Your Aim

When men and women have something important to do in the world they deal in facts. In their personal lives they deal mostly in impressions. In all their practical activities – what they call the really important things – they insist on having an aim. They run their businesses to make a profit, run a race to win. Every move is related in some way to an aim. What is the aim of your personal life? To be happy? Happiness, fulfilment, peace cannot be aims – they are experienced now or they do not exist.

When happiness is thought of as an aim it is a self-deluding impression, a word we use to hide the fact that our many personal aims are actually opposed to each other, impossible of attainment. To strive for happiness is wishful thinking.

For example, to be a loving partner and to amass money are two common aims. Can a loving partner devote his or her time to amassing money? No one can amass money by being home on time for meals or relaxing with their partner and family at weekends. There is an obvious conflict of aims. To achieve one aim, the other has to be neglected. To try to serve both aims the person will have to neglect both, split themselves – and this is nagging discontent.

To live with unhappiness or discontent we have to deceive ourselves. We cannot deceive ourselves with facts so we use impressions – half-truths – to justify to ourselves and others our unjustifiable personal conflict. This is not easy to see because everyone imagines it does not apply to them.

Ordinary man has so many shifting aims that they diffuse into aimlessness. Most of his aims add up to the aim of defending what he thinks he knows. His days are spent arguing, speculating, asserting and agreeing or not agreeing with what happens or is said, or they are spent in being indifferent. Because there is no going forward in this, no direction, his life becomes a drifting compromise with whatever circumstances happen to be thrown up. The result is frightening boredom or massive escapism. So he rushes for his morning newspapers, the television, the radio, the telephone, the pub and his friends – anything to fill the vacuum. Take away the Sunday papers or television and his day is demolished.

Long ago man convinced himself that the newspapers and all the rest are absolutely necessary, not understanding that they are habitual crutches supporting his aching emptiness. How else could he explain why such superficial experiences account for so much of his delight in living?

•

Your problem is that for personal happiness you rely on objects outside yourself which invariably disappear or change and cause you unhappiness.

For practical success or achievement you insist on action. What action can you perform to replace your habitual dependence on newspapers and things outside yourself – without interfering with anything? Meditation. The observation of yourself, the knowing of yourself. This is the never-ending action within all other action that depends on nothing but yourself.

Observe the difference between dealing in facts
and dealing in impressions.

Notice how in one way or another you announce
your likes and dislikes.

> *Oh, I love it . . .*
> *. . . No, no I don't like . . .*
> *I just hate these . . .*

Look and see what relevance your likes and dislikes
have to the matter in hand.

When you feel unhappy
or hard-done-by,
or even when you're just huffing and puffing,
ask yourself where the compromise is.

What's the compromise?

Try to get through today without talking about the past.

Don't feel bad when you fail.
See that the world is made of the past
and just observe yourself contributing to it.

Situation: a social occasion.
You're with a group of friends
and everyone is telling their story.

Refrain from telling yours
and see how it feels.

There is something you do habitually
that is a waste of energy
– and you know it.

Identify what it is.

> *I will not do that today.*
> *I give it up now.*

Give it up now
every time it starts.

Deprive yourself of the newspaper and television.
Just for a day or so.
Go without your usual entertainments.
Instead, give more time to yourself.

And for these couple of days
go into meditation as often as you can.
Aim at least to double your usual period of stillness.

LESSON TEN

Signs of Deepening Awareness

In the deeper, stiller states of meditation it is not unusual for your own higher consciousness to speak to you. It speaks from within, energetically, and may or may not speak in words. The communication will always be one of truth or wisdom, the imparting of knowledge that you know you did not know. It will amaze you.

You should write down or record what is imparted as soon as possible. The experience itself may be so intense and personal that you may feel the reality of it could never be lost. That is the truth – but the truth cannot be remembered.

The reality passes so quickly that very often doubt immediately sets in. Doubt is the mind's reaction to anything it does not understand. Doubt is thought. So you begin to think the experience was imagination. But do not doubt it. If you feel it happened, it happened. And do not build on it with your imagination.

You should not doubt your insights. Nor should you act on them. Observe the truth of them by holding the energy without thought, and in this way allow the energy to work in you. If you are meant to do something you will do it without thinking about it. This will preserve the developing inner silence in which the energy of self-knowledge works. And it will protect you from the possibility of acting out of your imagination.

Doubt soils the purity of the space and silence that your consciousness uses to reach you. Do not allow doubt to twist the space you have worked so hard to make.

●

You may see colours in meditation. These appear against the closed eyelids and often move in spirals. Blues and purples are most common as they are the basic colours of developing stillness, silence and self-discovery. All colours, however, have a positive meaning and should be observed without drawing conclusions. The energy of the colours will inform you without your mind being necessarily aware of receiving anything. What you are meant to know, you will know.

Sometimes sitting in meditation the eyeballs may tend to roll up into the forehead. Or the spine may suddenly stiffen and the head snap or roll back. These are signs of the rising of the kundalini energy which occurs as the mind becomes stilled and more silent.

The kundalini energy also causes pain in the head and it is not unusual for it to have been doing so before a person thinks about starting formal meditation. (Meditation is merely the conscious perception of a process that is going on unconsciously to some extent in everyone.) The kundalini pain occurs mostly in the back of the head and neck. Ordinary tension also causes pain here so it is not always possible to distinguish which is which until you rid yourself sufficiently of tension. Meditation does this in time.

As progress continues and the kundalini energy rises, the most uncomfortable and persistent pains are likely to be in the eye sockets and in the forehead over the eyes. It is here that the energy works on destroying the monkey-mind's attachment to the memory cells so that stillness can eventually come. The energy travels up the spine and while resistance to it persists in the neck and head, aches and pains will occur.

•

Isolated patches of heat in different parts of the body are not uncommon. This again is the energy at work. Eventually it has to work through the entire body, transforming it to accommodate more consciousness.

Sometimes in meditation you may observe yourself smiling for no apparent reason. This is your body's response to the incoming energy that is freeing it of tension.

Tears for no reason are also likely – another sign of inner change going on.

There are periods of aridity and dryness. This is when nothing is happening and you feel you are not only failing to make progress but are further behind than when you began. That is certainly not true. But it is the feeling. It has to be gone through and borne steadfastly. Some people feel an ugliness that makes them actually despise themselves. These conditions will pass and may be followed by finer perceptions and new experiences.

•

Other signs often found in people who have begun to meditate seriously include:

− A switch in reading interests from fiction to fact. An interest in archaeology or history, especially relating to ancient times.

− A tendency towards a meatless diet, pure food and semi-vegetarianism. A distaste for eggs and milk.

− A noticeable intolerance of violence or gossip.

− The need to sleep without a pillow, lying on the back.

− Headaches, including migraines.

− An excessive emphasis on personal cleanliness.

− A desire for a taste that is never satisfied.

− Mute discontent that nothing imaginable can subdue.

− Days of deep sighing for no apparent reason.

− And most significant, periods of sorrow without morbidity, or weeping without unhappiness, with no apparent cause. This is due to an increasing sensitivity to the predicament of all things in existence.

•

The body is your vehicle of awareness and you have to learn to 'read' it or you will miss the reality and truth of life. That is why in this meditation you practise and develop body consciousness.

Some people have been meditating unsuspectingly for years. The housewife who has to lie down each day and is refreshed by her own stillness without sleeping, might be one of them. But as you have now learned, meditation is not just relaxation; it is a continuing process of bringing more and more awareness into every part of yourself, constantly refining your perception.

In this meditation you practise and deepen the awareness of your body as the feeling of its sensation within, and that brings increasing stillness into the restless mind.

Use every situation and circumstance
to strengthen your meditation.

'Read' the sensation of your body.
Wherever you are in the world
and whatever's going on,
read what you're feeling.

That is reality.

Go into meditation.
Be still.

Lift the corners of the mouth
so that there is a slight smile on the lips.

Do this even if you don't feel like smiling.

The energy of the smile is within your body
and you are going to release it.

Feel the smile in your hands,
across the rib-cage,
in the belly.

There is warmth, joy in the body.

Life is good.

Don't fall into habits and routines
when you meditate.

> *Stillness is always fresh*
> *and of this moment.*

Don't look for experiences.
Don't try to repeat them.
And don't despair when there is lack of experience.

> *The truth cannot be remembered.*

Something is happening.
Don't doubt whatever happens.
As there is change within
so your life without will change.

> *Real change always comes on time.*

Repeat any of the exercises in this book
as you are moved to do them.

Persevere
but don't let meditation become a chore.

Give up all techniques as soon as possible.
Meditation – stillness – is not a technique.

Stillness is the way.

WHAT COMES NEXT . . .

In the ten meditation lessons just concluded – your foundation course – you have been shown how to approach stillness within by working through the resistance and interference of the thinking mind. By starting to master the mind you have started to dissolve the false in you.

Your meditation will become more advanced and be an indispensable function of your daily life. As you go on you will have to deal with the deep-seated source of much of your thinking – the emotion that has accumulated in you and that you are holding on to. You will have to work through your past to become your presence.

To confront you consciously with the deeper levels of yourself, I have written and recorded a tape – 'Start Meditating Now'. And an intensive course covering all aspects of meditative work on the spiritual path is to be found in my book 'Stillness is the Way'.

●

Your self-discovery has only just begun. Life will be your teacher.

There are three ways of learning how to perceive truth. The first is life. The second is by being with or questioning a person who sees life as it really is – a true spiritual teacher, guru or master. The third way is through books and recordings by such a person. The latter two ways are lesser parts of the sublime teacher, life. When you listen to a master or read his books you are accepting a substitute for life. Every book ever written on truth should be burned and everyone who knows what he is saying should never speak again – but when this happens, all men will be free. And that cannot happen until man no longer needs to read books and no longer needs to listen to other men – when he receives his full experience of life out of Life which is himself. Then men who know will never again have to corrupt the purity of silence with words which cannot tell the truth.

The philosophy and religion sections of public libraries are filled with speculative and imaginative writings and very little truth. How to distinguish between them is a problem until you develop discrimination. When this faculty appears you will find yourself discarding the commentaries and opinions of others on the great teachings and going direct to the teachers' words.

Go to the great sages – for example Krishnamurti, Meher Baba, Ramana Maharshi, among others. Read the Bhagavad Gita, an ancient and potent work describing the way of things, and Thomas à Kempis' 'The Imitation of Christ' – a beautiful work for the devotional temperament, especially helpful when the pressure of suffering begins.

Every teacher must be exceeded as quickly as possible. The

teaching must be absorbed as oneself. While you ever have to quote another you do not know the truth. The truth is not stored in any quotation. It is not kept in the memory. It is not in the brain. The brain is only the instrument we use to perceive what is true in our experience of the world. The truth is always found in life itself.

Man looks for truth in life as though life were something separate from himself, as though truth were stored in objects. Truth is in the relationship between objects and ourselves. It is a word for the true experience of them. If we do not see the object as it is, we will not see the truth of it. If we do not see ourselves as we are, we will not know the truth of ourselves.

Man goes wrong by memorising and repeating quotations such as 'God Is Love'. The truth is not in the quotation. It is in the experience of God Is Love in yourself. You may say you do not know this in your experience. Through meditation as the practice of stillness you are already on your way to it.

God, Love and Life are one and the same. They are the truth – the truth that you can realise for yourself; because they are the truth of yourself.

THE AUTHOR AND THIS BOOK

Editor's note

Barry Long was born in Australia in 1926 and led a convent-ional life until around the age of 30 he began to ask the fundamental questions that inspire all spiritual seekers: What is the purpose of my life? What is death? What am I – really?

Totally preoccupied with the search for truth, in 1964 he abandoned career and family and went to India. It was not a guru he was searching for; he has never associated with other teachers or teachings. He sought the elusive truth of life; in solitude, facing the pain of loss. Alone in the foothills of the Himalayas, he passed through 'the mystic death', a spiritual turning point which brings knowledge of man's essential immortality.

The ensuing clarity of mind and inner stillness were soon applied to a new vocation; he must help others find their own way to the truth. With that inspiration, in a few weeks 'Meditation - A Foundation Course' was written. The ten lessons distil all that he had discovered up to that time, expressed with the freshness and simplicity of his new understanding and tempered by the practical, straightforward common sense of his Australian upbringing.

He brought the original manuscript to London, along with other writings, to get them published; but in 1966 no commercial publisher was interested. The manuscript circulated in a private edition until 1982 when it was issued for sale as a staple-bound pamphlet in a few specialist London bookshops. In 1986 a revised edition was printed with an appendix including all the exercises he had been using in his more recent teaching. That edition of the book eventually reached out to thousands of people around the world.

The history of the book follows the history of its author. In the late 1960's his exceptional qualities as a man of truth were known only to a small circle of friends. By 1982 he was teaching a group in London, and for four years gave regular meditation classes there. In 1986, now well-known as a spiritual teacher in England, he moved back to Australia to live and teach in his native land. From 1990-93 he travelled extensively, giving seminars in Europe and America, and is now recognised as a spiritual master and world teacher.

In the present edition the exercise sections have been integrated with the lessons. There are a few new exercises and minor revisions of the text. Barry Long's teaching moves on, as the truth of the moment is always moving, but the Course remains a true foundation for self discovery and enquiry into the fundamental questions of life.

Also by Barry Long

START MEDITATING NOW
An audio cassette of instruction, written and spoken by
Barry Long, using the same straightforward approach as in
The Foundation Course, but going a little further into the dark-
ness of inner space. Listening to the voice of the teacher brings a
different quality to your meditation and the tape is recommended
as a way of bringing fresh energy or new commitment to your
work with the book. The power of stillness you have now attained
is used to deal with the root causes of restlessness and emotional
pain. More attention is given to the release of tension and the
dissolution of the emotions that rise from the subconscious
levels of the self, touched on in Lessons Three and Seven.
Recorded in 1983, the tape has been digitally re-mastered and
runs for 82 minutes.

STILLNESS IS THE WAY
As you have learned, continued practice of meditation takes
you deeper and deeper into stillness and self-knowledge. It
opens up a way of being that permeates every aspect of life.
This is demonstrated in *Stillness Is The Way*, a documentary
account of an intensive meditation course given by Barry Long
in London in 1984. As you read, you participate. You join the
seven students as they go through various stages of advanced
practice. Each individual's experience is seen with a universal
perception. Almost every aspect of Barry Long's teaching at that
time is encapsulated. The book ends where meditation ends,
giving access to the state of pure being.

KNOWING YOURSELF

Barry Long encourages us to question the impressions we have about ourselves and distinguish between the true and the false. Written around the same time as *Meditation A Foundation Course* this book contains short challenging essays to further the process of self-separation begun in Lessons Three and Five.

WISDOM AND WHERE TO FIND IT

A book of five talks on self-discovery. Barry Long explains why we suffer and teaches a way to face the truth of life through meditation and self-observation.

ONLY FEAR DIES

One way or another we must confront the truth of life and it is invariably painful. Often it feels like dying, but in the process a new consciousness is born. This book of eight essays confronts us with Barry Long's perceptions of personality, parenting, politics and the perennial discontent of humanity.

TO WOMAN IN LOVE

A book of letters from women to Barry Long and his replies — an intimate record of the spiritual experience of woman as she faces the truth of love and learns to trust her innate stillness in all relationships. Barry Long's letters are honest, forthright, utterly unsentimental, and yet full of acknowledgement and love of woman.

Contact Addresses [1995]

AUSTRALIA ~ THE BARRY LONG CENTRE
Box 5277, Gold Coast MC, Queensland 4217,
Tel +61 (0)75 76 7665 Fax +61 (0)75 76 7641

ENGLAND ~ THE BARRY LONG FOUNDATION
42 North Street, Wiveliscombe, Somerset, TA4 2LA
Tel +44 (0)1984 623426 Fax +44 (0)1984 624446

UNITED STATES ~ THE BARRY LONG FOUNDATION
c/o PO Box 251, Cerrillos, NM 87010
Tel/Fax +1 800 487 1081

Barry Long's latest publications catalogue, mailorder details
and seminar booking information can always be obtained
via:

THE BARRY LONG FOUNDATION
BCM Box 876 London WC1N 3XX England
